THE GARO TRIBAL RELIGION

THE GARO TRIBAL RELIGION
BELIEFS AND PRACTICES

Paulinus R. Marak

Maulana Abul Kalam Azad Institute of Asian Studies, Kolkata

ANSHAH Anshah Publishing House

Published on behalf of Maulana Abul Kalam Azad Institute of Asian Studies, Kolkata. Views expressed are those of the author/ contributors and do not reflect the position of the Institute and s/he are solely responsible for any copyright violation.
(First published in India in 2005)

Rs. 950; US$ 31.70

ISBN: 978-81-8364-002-2

2023
PoD Impression

The Garo Tribal Religion
Beliefs and Practices

Published by:
ANSHAH PUBLISHING HOUSE
LG 18-19, Pankaj Central Market,
IP Ext., Patparganj, Delhi 110092
011 22235152/ 6152, 96500 28065
info@shiprapublication.com
www.shiprapublication.com

Preface

The Garos are one of the tribal Groups of India settled in Garo Hills and they practised their own ancient beliefs, which they have had from the time of their origin. This study deals with the religious beliefs and practices of the Garos in particular.

I have also tried to record my observations and experiences regarding aculturation. Though the majority of Garos have been converted to Christianity their ancient beliefs and practices are still embedded in their minds. In such a study there may be some deficiency or error for which I am responsible.

Paulinus R. Marak

Acknowledgement

This study is done under the research fellowship of the MAKAIAS in the North-East. I take this opportunity to thank Dr. Mahavir Singh, Director of the Institute for his support and cooperation. I am grateful to Prof. J.N. Phukan, Head of the Department of History for his guidence to complete the study. Lastly, but not the least, I am grateful to Dr. Milton M. Sangma, who helped me with all the necessary materials for the study.

Contents

I
Introduction

ORIGIN AND THE FINAL SETTLEMENT OF THE GAROS

Historical traces give us the knowledge that the Garos originally and according to their ethnicity and language belonged to the Great Bodo family. The Garos as a tribe descended from Tibeto-Burman race of the Tibeto-Chinese family.[1] They lived and inherited the land in north western China between the upper waters of Yang-tse-kiang and Ho-ang-ho. The Garos later migrated and spread all over the valleys of the Brahmaputra and the great rivers Chindwin, the Irrawady and the Mekong that flow towards the South.[2]

The migration of the Garos is analogous to that the most other aboriginal tribes of the Assam Valley, like the Kacharis, Rabhas, Meeches etc and was to quite distinctive from that of Khasis.

The Garos traditionally being from Tibet settled down in Koch Behar for about 400 years. Later on when they moved on to Dhubri, they were warmly received by the king. However, the king later began to feel insecure and suspicious about the behaviour of the Garos. Being scared of them, the King did not allow the Garos to settle down permanently. So, they moved towards Jogighopa, from where again they were compelled to flee towards south. When they moved towards Gauhati, they were maltreated there by the King. So they wandered and settled in the neighbourhood of Boko. This place was, however, infested with tiger-men.[3]

The Garos, therefore, moved to the Habraghat Pargana, presently in Goalpara District of Assam. According to Dr. Milton S. Sangma's opinion in his *History and Culture of the Garos*, it was in the course of this journey that the Garo tribes broke into different branches. The Garos seemed to have become rich and prosperous while in Habraghat Pargana. It is generally believed that a kingdom was also established and the prince Abrasen was said to be the first to reign over it. Abrasen's palace and capital was known as Sambol A·ding (*Sam* means herbs/bush, *bol* means tree and A·ding means hillock—the hillock of herbs and trees), a detached hill near Dakaitdol village near Goalpara town. About this time dissenssion took place among the Garos themselves, and probably this was the reason for the scattering of the Garos in different parts of the North-East and Bangladesh. Some of them set out on their travel (journey) again and entered the hills which are now called the Garo Hills. One group under the leadership of a Chief named Abong Noga wandered from place to place untill it finally settled on Nokrek, the highest peak of the Tura range.,[4] Gradually, batches of Garos entered the Garo Hills of Meghalaya from different parts and settled down in isolated villages for centuries.[5] There, isolated settlements were the results of the evolution of certain regional linguistic and cultural variations amongst them. Thus, based according their linguistic and cultural differences the Garos are divided into eleven groups, namely:

1. The A·kawes or A·wes
2. The Chisaks
3. The Duals
4. The Matchis
5. The Matabeng or Matjangchis
6. The Chiboks
7. The Rugas
8. The Garas or Ganchings
9. The Atongs
10. The Me·gams
11. The Am·bengs, (A·beng)

Now, the Garos occupy a prominent place in the tribal map of India. The Garos in India and outside India, exhibit certain characteristic features which are unique and not to be found among other tribal groups anywhere.

It must be mentioned that the origin of the Garos as the coherent tribal entity that they are now, is shrouded in the mist of history. The Garos now like themselves to be called only as "A·chiks" which means Garos. The origin of the very name 'Garo' is a subject of great controversy. According to Major Playfair the 'Gara' or 'Ganching' sub-tribe among the Garos first received their appellation of 'Garos' which was later extended to all the inhabitants of the hills. The present day name 'Garo' is a corrupt form of 'Gara'. Another theory states that the word 'Garo' is either a development from 'Dura' or a corruption of it, and which subsequently was used for the people inhabiting the hilly region to the South of the Goalpara district of Assam.[6] Today the educated Garos like to call themselves only as 'A·chik' rather than by their divisional names.

The Garos are also greatly clan conscious people. The clan or Maharism has an important role in the Garo Society. The clan among the Garos is known as 'Chatchi'. Originally there were only two main clans, viz., Sangma and Marak. Later on the maharis like Arengh and Shira and others came into existence. Today, every Garo belongs to either one clan or the other.[7]

Thus the study of the Garo Tribal Religion has to be carefully dealt with their linguistic and ethnic divisions from the stand point of Final Settlement.

Though the Garos practised their beliefs inherited from the grassroots of their origin this study is confined to after their settlement in Garo Hills where they have firmly developed their traditional beliefs and practice and which have continued to the present day.

II
Nature of the Garo Tribal Religion

THE PANTHEON

At the outset we find the characteristic of the Garo Tribal Religion as a belief in the existence of a supreme Being. The Garos generally believe in the existence of a multitude of benevolent and malevolent spirits.[8] Some of these spirits are good and some are evil. They are collectively called 'Mites'. All these 'Mites' are considered immortal by them[9]. The term Mites in Garo language comes from what we call 'Deities'. The tribal religion of the Garos is similar to the general tribal religion as it is animistic in their beliefs and practices. It consists of the components of the sacred beliefs, types of spirits, sacred geography, sacred specialists and sacred rituals and performances. It is an undisputed fact that the tribals are more at home with a God supreme Being and with things and events pertaining to the divine and supernatural than their non-tribal fellowmen. At this juncture, a word of caution is appropriate for those who tend to explain off the religious beliefs and rites of the tribals as being superstitious and stemning from ignorance. J.H. Hutton says, "...the beliefs held by the tribals are not mere imaginings of superstitious and untaught minds ...but the debris of a real religious system, a definite philosophy".[10] For tribals, belief in the existence of superhuman or supernatural powers is universally true.[11] In a similar way the Garos also base their beliefs on superhuman existences or supernatural experiences of certain day to day events, sudden phenomena, disease, death and the unexplainable.

Among the Garos the religious performances of the various rituals and sacrifices imply recognition of the supernatural powers that can be exercised by the spirits. These rituals or sacrifices are performed to secure the goodwill of the benevolent spirits and to avert the ill-will of the malevolent ones. So the realm of Garo religious beliefs and rites are really comprehensive. The Garo concept of religion is not limited to the sphere of tradition-bound beliefs alone; it is translated into action in their daily lives.

The Garos practise earnestly what they believe firmly. They are the people who are overawed by the divine; and their history has originated and developed in and around their firm belief in a personal and supreme Being who is deeply interested in them and concerned about their welfare.

The religious beliefs and practices as well as customs differ from region to region. Different forms of worship, sacrifices, rites and ceremonies are conducted differently by the divisional groups according to their culture, language and place in Garo Hills. However, the aim or goal to obtain the effect of sacrifice and grace by means of worship, sacrifice and rite is the same. The Garos also have different kinds of beliefs, faith and isms prevailing among them based on their sacred 'beliefs', where the type of the spirit depends on the form of the effect produced or the action by the supernatural powers. There are sacred places and symbolic articles or objects representing the different powers. Sacred specialists are the persons, usually the 'Kamal' (the Garo Priest) or the 'Nokmas' (the Garo chiefs) who propitiate the so-called Deity of the group concerned; and finally the sacred performances reflect the method of propitiation, rituals, worship, offering of sacrifices, incantations, enchantments, etc. adopted by the Garo religion.

Thus, the Garo religion as pantheistic. The mythology of the Garos is voluminous and as intricate as that of the Hindu.[12] They have no written record but only the memory to preserve it. And by oral education they pass on their traditional myths, beliefs and practices to the future generation.

III
Garo Deities and their Power and Function

The Deities in which the Garos believe are said to be present everywhere. Their places of dwelling are in the sky above, on the earth beneath, in the depths of water, rivers, pools, stones, trees, bamboo groves, in the dark caverns, recesses of mysterious mountains, the shrubs, sticks and stones are also considered as the dwelling places of some spirits.[13] The Garos consider these deities as immortal. These deities are assigned some special powers and functions. To some of these spirits is attributed the power of creation of the world, to others the control of natural phenomena, and the destinies (human goal) of man from birth to death are governed by a host of divinities whose anger must be appeased by sacrifice, rituals and whose good offices must be entreated in like manner.[14] The mythological beliefs of the Garos are voluminous. Each spirit is known by several names bearing the teknonymous affixes for father and mother though they cannot actually perceive the deity which they think causes diseases, saying 'mite doka' or 'smite chika', 'the deity or spirit bites'. When they are enquired or asked they say that they cannot know where they are and what they look like. They cannot identify their gender. They simply believe that when some sicknesses, ill-omens, diseases, misfortunes befall upon them, they are caused by some particular 'mite' or deity.[15] However, they believe to have the idea of particular deity or mite by the symptoms of the disease which indicates which spirit is causing it, thus allowing those concerned to choose the proper kind of sacrifice.

THE PRINCIPAL GARO DEITIES

TATARA-RABUGA

He is regarded as the creator. At his command the world was made by two lesser spirits, namely, Nostu-Nopantu and Machi. He is regarded as the greatest of all the spirits. He has a special mission to bring welfare to human beings, to cure them from diseases like Kalazar and fevers.[16] The Garos call him by about one hundred and sixty names, of which the following are some of the names mentioned, Tatara-Rabuga, Bisikrom Bidatare, Rabugama, Ranagama, Stura Pantura, A·ning Randinima, Ambi Mori, Dakdame, Rurime, Dakgipa Rugipa, Aiti, Biati, Korabok Korapin, Maresu Marebok, Dingipa, Babra, Ba·rangipa, Chitragipa, Nirikgipa, Sandigipa, Ja·rikgipa, Ja·sangipa, Janggini Nokgipa, Jamani Biambi, Pattigipa, Ra·rongipa, Sualgipa, Imbagipa, Mikbergipa, Mitdakgipa, Ja·ragipa,

Ja·chitgipa, Rakkigipa, Nirokgipa, Chijanggiko Ripinggipa, Chichrigipa Rakkigipa, Chijanggiko Kangipa, Chichriko On·gipa, Jikmite Gosai, Ma·gipa Jagring.[17]

A sacrifice to him is an expensive matter, a bull, a goat and a fowl must be slaughtered in his honour; liquor and rice are also to be provided for the worshipers. The ceremony lasts for two days.[18]

SALJONG

The Garos regard Saljong as one of the greatest among the spirits. He is the giver of all materials to human beings and all other living beings on earth, in water and above the earth. The sun represents him. He is also the god of fertility. The Garos worship him with great reverence because he is the spirit who is responsible for all the crops from the time of germination to the harvest. Whatever harvest is reaped is due to his favour and mercy.[19] The great festival of the year, the 'Wangala', is celebrated in his honour after the harvest. Wangala is also known as the Thanksgiving offering festival. A sacrifice is offered to him in the fields before the village festival begins. A cock is killed, its blood is sprinkled on the sacrificial altar, a little liquor is poured out on the ground in front of it, and the worshipers then return to the village for the Wangala rejoicings.

The spirit is also known by the names Tengsugipa-Tengtotgipa, Salgira, Salgra and Rengra-Balsa.[20]

NOSTU-NOPANTU

He is the creator of the earth. With the help of another spirit named Machi, he fashioned the earth at the command of Tatara-Rabuga. No sacrifice is required to offer to these two deities because they are harmless to any human beings.[21]

CHORABUDI

He is a benign spirit and the protector of crops. Before partaking of the first fruits of the season, such as the Indian corn, millet and melons, a small quantity of some of these is always given as an offering to him. The sacrifices made for him are for pain in the ears and boils. He is the servant of Tatara-Rabuga, and when the latter is offered a sacrificed, a pig has to be offered to Chorabudi also.[22]

GOERA

He is regarded as the deity of strength. He is the causer of thunder and lightning and prayed to for health and strength after long illnesses; sacrifices are made to him at the foot of a tree. A pig, a fowl or a duck are used for the sacrifices. If a tree has been blasted by lightening, it is said that Goera has struck it, and a sacrifice must be offered at the foot of that tree in order that harm may not come to the dwelling houses in the vicinity.[23] Goera used to blast the trees, men or animals with a flat stone which is called 'Rongpra' in Garo. It is believed that the Rongpras have strong medicinal values.[24]

KALKAME

He is Goera's brother. He is the spirit who holds in his hands the lives of all men. He guarantees safety from dangers from wild animals, aquatic animals and all kinds of dangers and diseases. For his benevolent nature people offer him sacrifices to please him. He is prayed to in the A·song tata or A·songroka ceremony, and is entreated to keep the people of the village safe from all dangers of the forest during the coming year. The A·song or sacrificial stones are erected in his honour and the evils are driven away in his name. A goat or a cock is offered to this spirit and the offering is made on the sacrificial stones which are smeared with blood of the victim.[25]

SUSIME

Susime and Salgira are said to be brothers. Susime is associated with the moon. As the giver of both good and bad things to all mankind, she can blind people or lame them, but the diseases caused by this deity can be cured by sacrifice.[26] Susime is also expert in instigating people to quarrel. That is why they try to please her by offering sacrifices of a pig, a fowl and some liquor and by enchantment.[27]

ASIMA-DINGSIMA

She is the mother of Susime. She is not attributed to possess any power and therefore is not sacrificed to, but a superstition exists that it is unlucky to pronounce her name as it is feared that she may not like to be mentioned. The Garos call upon her by the names Norekbak-Norekdim, Sonakale-Kaburanchi and Mikronggitok-Ki.sanggitok.[28]

TONGRENGMA

Tongrengma, a female deity has the power to cause ailment to mankind. When she troubles a man, the sphincter comes out and the patient suffers from pain. A fowl has to be sacrificed near a river or a stream to appease her.[29]

NAWANG

He is an evil spirit who devours souls of men on their way to the 'Balpakram', the 'Abode of Ghosts'—the Garo Purgatory. When a person dies, his dresses, ornaments and money are thrown away along with him so that he can offer them to the Nawang and can proceed on his journey. He also endeavors to devour living men, and in order to do so he roams the world over, sometimes in human from and sometimes in that of Maldendong, a mythical animal. He also causes pains in the stomach, vomiting diarrhoea and is often present at a man's death-bed ready to devour him when he is dead. A mortal carrying a weapon of iron is perfectly safe, but sometimes the demon borrows it, and can work his wicked way after throwing it to a distance.[30]

The Garos believe that the constellation of stars have powers and it represents a group of spirits. They possess power to give both good and bad things to man. The seasons and years are also under the control of one or the other spirits. Therefore, they used to sacrifice a pig, a cow, a goat, a fowl or a duck to them, so as to keep them in good humour and gain their favour.[31]

The stars which the Garos believe to represent some spirits are collectively known as Noringro-Nojingjo. The fourteen stars recognised by the Garos are given below :

Mangripe (Cassiopeia); Mirontek (Sirus); Do·sadil (The Pliades); Chapchore-Nonje (Castor and Pollux); Ja·tokani (Walking Stick); Do·sutat (Cock fighting); Aski Do·me (Comet); Menggo ripe (carrying of the cat); Wak ripe (Belt of onion); Mangganchi (Square of Pegasus); Matma ja·kol (The Milky Way); Pringprang (Morning star or Venus); Attamprang (Evening star or venus)

The above mentioned stars represent certain spirits and accordingly, the Garos have explanation for the power and function of each star.

IV
The Garo Priest (Kamal) and the Chief (Nokma)

THE NOKMA

In the ancient political system of the Garos, there existed the Nokma and the Village Council. The existence of the Nokma and the Village Council among the Garos was prior to the advent of the British who established the present political system.

DERIVATION OF THE WORD

The word 'Nokma', commonly means a 'rich man'. However, it has two literal meanings. First, "Nok" means a 'house' and 'Ma' is both an affix and a suffix, which is used in the context of 'big'. Thus, ethnologically, Nokma means a 'big house'. Though it is used to refer to the man of the house, it carries some meaning as the house of the Nokmas are generally bigger than other houses of the Village.

Secondly, the word 'ma' also means 'mother' and in this sense, it means the "mother of the house." Though it invariably refers to the man of the house, but since the man owns the house and the household property in the name of his wife and her clan, this ethnology also conveys some practical meaning. Thus, though the Nokma, that is, the man is theoretically the owner, the actual owners are his wife and her clan. As the head of the clan the Nokma is only a custodian of the lands and property of his wife and her clan.

FOUR KINDS OF NOKMAS AMONG THE GAROS

THE GAMNI NOKMA

He is a mere rich man of the village. One who becomes rich is regarded as the Gamni Nokma. However, he has no political power and authority.

THE GANA NOKMA

He is also a rich man of the village, but in order to gain social prestige and respect, performs the "gana ceremony" in which he gives sumptuous feast to all the people and dances round and round merrily in front of the assembled guests. To symbolise his recognition as the Nokma, he wears a thick metal ring round his elbow. Such a Nokma commands social respect from his co-villagers because of his wealth. However, he is devoid of political power.

THE A· KING NOKMA

The A·king Nokma holds a great power among the Garos. He holds title to the A·king land of the village community as head of the clan. He becomes the A·king Nokma by virtue of his marriage with the girl of the heiress and the senior of the house of the village.[32] As the head of the clan and as the custodian of the A·king land, he has important powers and functions. As such, the A·king Nokma is the only Nokma who has political and judicial authority.

Succession to A·king Nokmaship is subject to ordinary laws of inheritance through the system of Nokma (heiress), and Nokkrom (man married to an heiress). When entitled by the A·king Nokma they are recognised by the Government as Nokma. When they succeed to Nokmaship, their names are entered in the record of Nokmas by the Deputy Commissioners. At present the records are kept and maintained by the District Council.[33]

The A·king Nokma is recognised as the chief of the village as he has political, judicial and social status. Therefore, in order to pass on these powers as

Nokmaship, like any other Nokmas he looks for his own nephew, that is the son of his sister, to come and be his son-in-law and heir. Thus the nephew not only becomes the heir to the house and property but also succeeds to the 'headship' when his father-in-law dies. As a customary rule, a Nokma should be a member of the lineage and from the same village as the previous Nokma. Therefore, generally a succession of Nokmas are members of the one village and lineage by descent but can get the status of Nokma or head man in another village by virtue of being married to the girl who is successively chosen as heiress in the senior house of the village.[34]

In the case of the lack of a daughter, the female child or girl is adopted from the nearest relation or clan of the Nokma's wife as heiress and she together with her husband succeeds to the A·king land.

The A·king Nokma holds his Office through the right of the A·king which theoretically belongs to his wife and her clan. The office of the Nokma has the intrinsic importance from the point of view of the Garo organisation. The Nokma plays the leading role as the central figure in village activities and externally represents the village.

However, the position of the Nokma is very delicate. When he fails to function effectively, he may be dismissed by the villagers who, with all members of the lineage group, can dis miss him by proving his inefficiency in discharge of his duties. In connection to with this Milton S. Sangma gives a concrete example of a case of recent years: in the case of Rombagre the Nokma was dismissed due to this great failure to arrange for the performance of funeral service of his wife.[35]

The A·king Nokma also holds the power to possess the 'Kram', a Garo traditional drum which is endowed with supernatural power for which special sacrifices are required before making it. Kram is used only on special occasions such as funerals and some annual ceremonies of religious nature. No one can permanently possess it except the A·king Nokma.

The A·king Nokma also holds economic power without whose distribution the forest land cannot be cleared for jhum cultivation. He distributes the forest lands to the household villagers for cultivation according to the number of its members. This distribution is done on rotational basis every year. Nokma also gets his share in the same way as that of the other families. The Nokma, in theory, has no special advantages over commoners. In fact some of the Nokmas are even poorer than other ordinary villagers.[36]

As the Nokma is the centre of social and cultural activities within the village as well as outside, his expenses are high. The entertainment of visitors rests on his shoulders. It is the usual custom for visitors who have no kins in the village to stay at the Nokma's house and eat there. No other villager is allowed to keep any foreigners or strangers without any information and consent of the Nokma. If any one does so he is solely responsible for any unwanted or unexpected situations which may arise in the village. If any stranger or foreigner comes to any villager, he or she must lead the concerned person to the Nokma's house. And with his consent he or she may accept the persons as the guest or the stranger has to stay in Nokma's house till his mission is achieved. That is why Nokma's daily expenditure is higher than any other villager's.

Festivals, funerals and marriage ceremonies are conducted in the presence of Nokma. All the social and religious ceremonies are started from his house and concluded in his house. Therefore, it is his obligation to provide extra meals and drinks to the people. If the Nokma is poor, the responsibility is taken over by the second Nokma or fourth Nokma or even by the Gana Nokma. Likewise, if the Nokma is Christian, for certain activities in which the Nokma has to play a religious role, a wealthy and senior non-Christian husbandman, or the second Nokma, if he is not a Christian, is to take his role. When the wealthy man takes the place of a Nokma in a religious ceremony, such a man is addressed as the Gana Nokma.[37] Other than this the Nokma has to play a ceremonial role to mark important points in the annual cycle, such as cleaning the jungle, planting and harvesting, etc. On such occasions, the Nokma must act as ceremonial leader, performing sacrifices and reciting incantations to ensure vigour for the village. At many of these sacrifices, the Nokma is expected to provide the sacrificial animal himself. Though these brings a degree of prestige, but it is also a considerable economic burden for the Nokma. However, if the Nokma is really unable to furnish the animal, other villagers may assist him, but it is always preferable for the Nokma to provide it himself.[38]

Nokma receives one direct economic benefit from his title only when an outsider cultivates the land within his A·king land. It is only about Rupee one per plot, hence it is insignificant. Nepalis who have settled in the hills and who keep their cattle may pay the Nokma an a·wil fee. The Nokma also receives some share from the extraction fee called the Nokma's fee for certain forest and mineral products, like timber, bamboo, coal, etc.[39]

A·king Nokmas are also responsible for the peace and good administration, such as submission of reports on epidemics, natural phenomena, births or deaths or any unusual occurrences in their A·kings. Besides, he also regulates Jhum. Cultivation and participates with the villagers in all public and social works and religious functions. In ancient times, the Nokmas had to take the leadership in wars against the external invasions and towards the security of their villages.

In the settlements of disputes, the Nokmas try all cases of theft, injury to property, injury to persons not affecting life or limb, house-trespass and affronts, provided neither of the parties is a near relative of theirs or a foreigner. They punish by fine after proceedings are held in open Durbar. The decisions made in these durbars are final and put into execution at once.[40]

THE KAMAL NOKMA (THE GARO PRIEST)

He is a village priest. His sole power and functions are to conduct religious ceremonies. He has no any political power.

The Kamal or the Priest conducts various ceremonies such as birth ceremony and naming a child; marriage ceremony, funeral ceremonies, religious ceremonies in connection with jhumming and ailments, which will be discussed in details in the following chapters.

The Kamal is the Garo animist priest. The office of the priest is not hereditary, nor it is confined to any particular clan, for anybody may assume the duties who can commit to memory the necessary string of obscure sentences and incantations and can name series of names of the spirits, or who is better endowed than his neighbours with the power of divination.[41]

The Kamal's life has certain drawbacks, for his duties are often multifarious and unpleasant. He has to keep watch by the side of the dead for long hours, reciting tedious funeral dirges.

He is paid very little renumerartion, and in no way does the Kamal enjoy special privileges. He must work in the fields and grow his crops like the rest.

In modern times the Christian villages have their own well organised churches and Christian priests attend to the various religious ceremonies. The only way in which his lot is different from that of his neighbours is that he must devote his attention to the requirements of others, even at personal inconveniences.[42]

As such the post of the Kamal is not enviable one. Yet every village has its Kamal, without whom the normal life is not possible.

V
Religious Ceremonies in Connection with Jhuming

The ancient Garos are mostly agriculturists. The Garos have various religious ceremonies during the jhum cultivation as the jhuming is the most commonly practiced by the Garos.

The jhum cultivation is done by clearing the jungle and leaving it to dry for a month or more. When the thick shrubs and the trees are dried up; it is burned and the burnt field covered with blackened ash is ready for sowing the seeds and planting crops.

The garos have various religious ceremonies that they conduct periodically. There are about seven main ceremonies in connection with jhuming.

The first ceremony is *A·A O·PATA* or *JUMANG SIA* (little clearence of the plot of land for having a dream). Before a man decides to clear and cultivate a plot of land he consults the omen. A little portion of a plot of land in one corner is cleared and he consults the deity by chanting rituals. According to the story of creation it is believed that it was the deity Tatara Rabuga Stura Pantura who created the earth or ground and water. Then it was the deity Jipjini Jipjana who created the lives on the earth above and in the waters below. It was the Asima Dingsima Dramma Chisama Den·pema Den·jima, the spirit or deity, who created the trees and the shrubs. After all of this creation only the spirit Abetpa Ranggapa was assigned by Tatara Rabuga Stura Pantura to look after the whole creation.

Therefore, if any person without any consultation with this spirit clears the plot of land the assigned spirit will be wrathful and he may even cause any illness or death.[43]

So, after clearing a portion of the land at a corner in consultation with the deity he goes home. At night, if he has a bad dream he abandons the land and looks for another plot of land where the omens are more favourable. This ceremony is performed by every individual without festivities. In this ceremony no animal or fowl is killed.

DEN· BILSIA FESTIVAL

Literally, the word 'Den·' means 'cut' and 'bilsi' means "year". This festival is celebrated to mark the completion of the clearing of the new jhum field. During this ceremony, as believed by the Garos, the evil spirits or the filths are also driven out so that the spirit of the crop may come and dwell in the new field of jhuming. The deity of the crops Rokimema will come and dwell in the new field only when the sins and the unclean conscience of the villagers are purified. The ceremony Den·bilsia is performed in such a way as to invoke the deity-Rokime (deity of the crops) that she may come to dwell in their new field and bless and look after their whole crop. This ceremony is held sometime in the first week of February and at the footpath side of the villager preferably near the house of Nokma. For this ceremony a dog is mostly used but a goat also is killed depending on the economic condition. In the morning of this festival day, the villagers gather together to built an elaborate altar and try to complete it by mid-day. The Nokma, then, sacrifices a goat at the altar invoking the help of the deities for the healthy growth of the crops. In the afternoon, all the villagers join and community feast begins where all the villagers dance, eat and drink the rice beer in the Nokmas house. This festival is also known as Rama Krita, or A·a Bakchata or Wa·cheng Balroroa.

A· GALMAKA

Having cut the jungle and let it dry, the entire field is set on fire. On the following day, the first sacrifice to the deity of the field takes place. It is called

A·galmaka. For this sacrifice a fowl or a dog is offered by killing and sprinkling the blood on the particular spot of the field specially chosen, preferably in the middle of the field. This ceremony is conducted by all individuals in their own new fields. During the sacrifice the deity of the crop-Rokimema is specially invoked, and the blood of the killed fowl is sprinkled and the rice beer is poured out for her and some enchantment also is spelled out. All the villagers specially prepare for this sacrifice and await eagerly for this occassion.

Every villager goes to his own field with luxuriant food and the chu dikka (the big earthen degchi containing beer or vodka). After the sacrifice to the deity Rokimema and offering her the best rice beer - chu bitchi, they eat and drink. This is followed by scattering and sowing of the seeds. After sowing is completed, every one returns to the village and while returning they wish well their fellow cultivators and share their own drinks. On their way to the village they also play with black asah of the burnt field by rubbing each others' faces as in the Holi festival celebrated by the Hindus. They return to the village happily and in the evening all of them drink and feast in the house of the Nokma. After that the elderly people visit all the houses of the village during the day after eating and drinking in every house while the younger folks visit them at night. The feasting ends by eating, drinking and dancing for several days and nights.[44]

A· SIROKA

The Garos do not abandon the cultivated land. They cultivate the same jhum land in the next year along with the new ones. For this a particular festival is celebrated in connection with planting of rice and other cash crops. Literally, 'A·siroka' means clearing of the ground and it is celebrated after clearing of the jungle in the old fields. This sacrifice is performed in order to inaugurate the planting of crops invoking the aid of deities for bringing gains and sunshine at proper time.

This festival begins with the slaughter of a cow purchased jointly by all the villagers and the distribution of its meat. Nokma then offers a sacrifice. On the following day every villager takes rest and no one is allowed to go to the fields. The main ceremony takes place on the next day. Every cultivator sacrifices an egg and the richer people sacrifice a fowl or a pig and call upon Saljong (the sun-god) to witness the sacrifice and bless the planting of rice and other crops.

The villagers who are less wealthy and cannot afford to perform their sacrifices are invited by the rich people and their clans to attend the sacrifices followed by luxuriant dinner and drinks. After this sacrifice they take rest and then attend to their work in the fields as usual.

A·KRITA OR MEJAK SIMA

Literally A·krita means "sacrifice for the land", 'A·a' means 'land' and 'krita' means 'sacrifice'. This sacrifice is performed mostly when the crops in jhum land have grown up especially when the crops come up with green leaves. The aim of sacrifice is an offering to the deity of crops so that she may protect the crops from every possible destruction by the insects, moths, animals, failure of rain, etc. The Garos also believe that whatever their works are done without the blessing and divine assistance, such works are not fruitful. In order to get fruitful harvest and protection of the crops by the divine assistance this particular sacrifice is performed.

This sacrifice is conducted in the month of May when the crops in the land bloom with the green leaves. This sacrifice is performed near the footpath of the village. For this sacrifice an altar is built by clearing the surroundings. Some home-made articles like broom, traditional basket etc. are placed at the altar. A stone is also erected where instead of rice sand is placed signifying that harvest will be fruitful. The Priest uses the bow made from bamboo and he carries some water with him. While the Priest gets ready with all the necessary articles for sacrifice, other villagers go about their own jhuming lands and shout out and chase the evil spirits which destroy the crops and come to the altar and fill up the traditional basket with mud, shouting that the witch or the evil spirit has entered. The Priest also sprinkles water on the altar by the broom and ties up the basket shouting that evil spirit has entered in it. He, then, keeps the basket hanging in the shrubs planted at the altar.

In this sacrifice a pig is slaughtered and the blood is sprinkled on the altar. When the Priest finishes the sacrifice with enchantment, all the villagers, who take part in the sacrifice, get involved in cooking and conclude the sacrifice by eating and drinking the traditional 'chu' or 'wine'.[45]

RONGCHU GALA OR WANNA STITA GURI JANGGIA

This is the thanks-giving ceremony offering the first fruits to the deity Saljong. The Garos also believe that they should first offer to the deity the products of their fields. Without first offering to the deity - Saljong, they don't eat anything. In this ceremony they pluck the rice and flatten it. 'Rongchu' means 'flat rice' which is soaked in the water and then with some enchantment and invoking Saljong that she may come back to their fields in future and bless them again. The soaked flat rice is strewn in the stream nearby the village. The Nokma performs this sacrifice. On the day of this ceremony the Nokma takes the flat soaked rice early in the morning before anybody gets up and strewns the flat rice in the stream.[46] Then he comes home and pours out the first prepared rice beer of the first harvest to the Misi Susime, the deity of rice and millets ('misi' means 'millet'). 'Susime' the one who blesses every harvest. No one of the village does this act of thankgiving before the Nokma performs the ceremony of thanksgiving. In this ceremony 'the rice powder' called 'ginde' is also strewn and spotted all over the posts and walls of the house, at the main pillar of the house. Other products of the field like lime, sugarcane, taro, manioc, gourds, etc. are also offered before actual harvest by the villagers. This ceremony then is followed by eating, drinking and beating of drums and gongs in every house of the village. Mostly fish or dried fish is considered as proper food during this ceremony.[47]

This ceremony signifies the unbroken covenant between the human beings and the deity. To symbolise this the Nokma ties a knot with a newly stripped skin of a particular tree (a kind of tree instead of the jute which is used by the garos) at his house. This also symbolises that other festivals or ceremonies in connection with jhuming still remain. This particular act of covenant is found in every Nokma's house of the village. Therefore, this ceremony is also called "Wanna Stita Guri Janggia" in Garo, which means "an act of covenant with the deity of the crops".

After this ceremony the Garos harvest the best part of rice usually grown in the middle of the field surrounding the Jamadal or the resting hut of which the best grains are then brought to the house with special chantings accompanied by incensing. These best grains are then kept with special care as the seeds for the next cultivation. This is a small ceremony performed by the individuals and called as "Ja·pang ra·a" meaning "taken for the seed".

Sometime towards the month of September, after the harvest, a ceremony is performed in order to thank the spirits and the deities for the harvest. This is an occassion for young folk to shout in a peculiar way called 'Ahaia'. This is the ceremony during which every Garo breaks the abstinance by beating the drums, gongs or shouting ahaia, while the rice is ripening. They also don't eat some crops before the ceremony of 'A·krita'.

In this way Garos maintain their peaceful relationship with the supernatural beings which surround them. If they do not maintain such relationship they believe that the deities or the spirits may be offended and as a result any kind of suffering may be brought to the transgressor. This is a salutary attitude which allows each man to conduct his behaviour with little fear of moral disapproval from others and helps to keep the Garos from getting too worried about the horrible effects of some offence to the spirits.[48]

So, in Ahaia ceremony they start beating drums and shout. However, certain religious principles pertaining to the individuals, behaviour are always kept, and the annual festivals are designed to preserve harmony with the supernatural. Ahaia and Wangala are the ceremonies which mark the significant stages in the annual cycle, and they provide occasions for most joyous celebrations of the year. Even in ahaia the best kind of food is prepared with sumptuous curries of fish, dried fish, crab or fowl; and all the young folk shout, dance, eat and drink making all kind of sounds in the village for many days and nights.

WANGALA

This is the greatest festival of all. All the Garo tribal religious people celebrate this festival. This celebration is held after the harvest in October. This is the most festive observance of the year and combines religious sacrifice with much conviviality. The cost of the entertainment falls principally on the Nokma of the village, who has to provide a pig to be eaten by the guests and plenty of rice-beer.

Each village sets its own time and so there two or three weeks during which Wangala is celebrated in one or two villages. This festival is observed to honour and offer sacrifices to the Saljong—the greatest deity of the Garos.

A particular day is fixed by the village Nokma well ahead of the time for the Wangala festival in order to provide ample time to everyone to make elaborate preparations. Everybody makes hectic preparation—

buying the best cows, clothes, ornaments and other necessaries from the market, so that they may provide good accomodation to their guests. On the preceeding day of the Wangala festival, the village is busy with slaughtering of cows and in the distribution of its meat. Liquors have already been prepared in large quantity in every household, especially of the Nokmas and wealthy people. Even the poorest of poor some how affords to prepare atleast five to six dikkas (Garo's big earthen pot for preparing rice-beer).

The Wangala festival begins in the Bachelors' house, where the young men act as hosts to all the villagers. The youths serve beer, rice and beef curry to the guests. The beef curry is mostly cooked with rice powder and that also with soda or sodium carbonate prepared by burning the remains of mustard stems, bamboos or banana trunks. All these are burnt, the ash is soaked and left for filtering through a net woven from bamboo strips artistically. When liquids is collected in a jar it is ready to substitute the soda that we get in the market. Sometimes the meat is simply cooked dry with chillies, ginger and soda which is called 'kapa' in Garo. Every foreign visitor or non-Garo likes this preparation which is prepared by all the Garos with all kinds of meat. Of course, the Garos have respect for other religions and so they do not serve the beef curry to non-Garos or anybody without first consulting them. The ancient Am·beng Garos are poor in cooking any curry with oil or spice. Their cooking and food habits are simple. With the advance of education and modernisation every Garo has now improved a lot in cooking skills.

When the evening festivity is over with few dances the real Wangala ceremony begins the next day with the "Chu-Rugala" ceremony (chu - liquor, and rugala - pour out). The Nokma acts like the priest. He begins the ceremony by worshipping the various deities and spirits with enchantment and incensing in his house, the house of the Kamal-Priest, and then in the houses of the other villagers. All along with act of paying reverence to various deities and spirits while the drums, flutes and other traditional instruments are beaten rhythmically to which other villagers respond by mild and rhythmic dance. According to the custom hands are dipped the rice powder mixed with water by all the assembled people who make white hands and finger marks on the posts and walls of the house and on the backs of the guests.

The Nokma then by, spelling the words of gratitude by incantations invokes and worships deities and spirits specially mentioned during Wangala. The deities and spirits which are specially worshipped during Wangala are Rongdik Mite (Rongdik - big earthen pot, and Mite - spirit). This spirit is believed to be female and resides in the pot where rice is kept. This worship is made in the presence of women.

The concept of belief in this spirit is analogous to the Hindu goddess 'Lakshmi'. In the evening the Kamal (priest) pays a special reverence by tying a cotton thread round the neck of the rice-pot with three lumps of cotton hanging round it. The priest then invokes the spirit with chanting of prayers and offers sacrifices by killing three hens with a dao in front of the pot. The blood is sprinkled all over the pot and on the cotton lumps, and the feathers are tied to the pot. All this takes place within the room. According to the belief of the Garos this spirit is the goddess of wealth and specially revered and is worshipped by the ladies. Other important sacrifices to the deities like Nokni mite or Pakmana Do·tata (the spirit of the house); Krongna Do·tata the sacred post, (krong - post); Kram Do·tata (spirit of the drum); Akom, Miwa Do·tata - sacrifice to the gong, the bell, Nagra Do·tata - a flat drum; Ang·ke Do·tata - the sacrifice to the crab; are serially done one by one within the house. Cocks, hen and crabs are sacrificed followed by sprinkling the blood and strewing the feathers.[49]

After due respect and worship of the spirits are over in the house of the Nokma, the actual 'chu rugala' or 'pouring out' of the best liquor ceremony begins. With beating of the drums and gongs and playing of various musical instruments liquor is poured out on all the places where worship has been made. The Nokma brings out the pot of liquor and offers a glass of it to the priest. After the priest has drunk, all the villagers assembled are allowed to drink. The Nokma supplies the entire drink required during 'chu rugala' ceremony. All the youth, women and children also drink and make merry from one house to the other. The guests and the members of other villages who join the festival are also given sumptuous drinks and can enjoy riotously.

When the drinking is over, the priest and the Nokma wear the traditional dresses called 'gando' (a small cotton cloth) the turban, a ring of bell metal at elbows and a ring bell metal at the wrist. With such traditional dress they dance round the fireplace inside the house of Nokma, after which all the villagers are also allowed to dance till late hour at night.

After the dance ceremony "Sasat So·a" ceremony is performed. The cooked rice is strewn in the house of Nokma. The strewing of cooked rice signifies symbolically the falling of hailstones during storm and heavy rainfall represents the monsoon. The Nokma invokes the spirit to bless them with such rainfall in their agriculture. Then he incenses the house and makes the inner house smoky with the incense. This "Sasat So·a" or incensing is significant, it represents the gathering of clouds before a big storm. The Nokma himself beats the 'dani' a kind of traditional instrument and while dancing invokes the rain by chanting of words.

All the villagers, men and women, girls and boys, and the children behind them; dance in accordance with the beating gongs, drums, playing of flutes, etc. wearing the traditional dresses, turbans and the cock-tail feather worn with turban. While the incensing is going on the drums are beaten non-stop; drinking and dancing also go on without stoppage. If the smoke of the incense fills the Nokma's house and blows through the ceilings they believe that the deity is happy with their performance and will bless them with heavy rainfall and good harvest even in the future.

When incensing and dancing are over at the Nokma's house, the son-in-law of the Nokma performs the incensing ceremony where all the villagers join, eat, drink and dance. When the 'Sasat So·a' ceremony is over the villagers dance, eat and make merry. The youth dance differently at the square and during this time they take the opportunity to select, choose and propose to the girls to be their life partners. If any of them likes to get married they duely inform their own parents and accordingly the Do·sia or the traditional Garo marriage ceremony is conducted by the Kamal or the Garo priest. With such pomps, sumptuous food and drink, they dance and end the 'Wangala Ceremony' which may last for even a week.[50]

VI
Religious Ceremonies in Connection with Ailments

Religious ceremonies in connection with ailments are quite unique from those of other tribals. Like any tribal performing sacrifice for the sick or ailing person the Garos also practice ceremonies and offer sacrifices for the sick as they believe that the sicknesses, diseases or bad omen falling upon them are due to their trespasses and disobedience against the law of nature and deities.

The word of sin is not known to the tribal Garos. They do not have a written code of laws to regulate their daily life either. However, it cannot be said that they are devoid of laws. In fact the Garos have too many laws which they observe and consider fully binding. The Garos have three specific words, which embody a complete programme of observances. The three simple specific words are 'Asimalja', 'Dakmalja' and 'Nima'.[51] These three words are enough for the Garos to observe the laws of nature and to bind their daily moral behaviour, because strictly speaking, a Garo always observes a code of conduct that abhors any act which may injure the feelings of any person in the society and honours those that maintain or restore peace therein. To a Garo, majority of the wrongs come under the category of torts.[52] The Garos only know that transgression of certain social and religious taboos involves supernatural punishment to the people. They have an idea of supernatural world that consists of the deities and spirits (mite) and the spirit of the dead—memang. Memang does not possess supernatural powers but may excite fears in the minds of the living and is always to be avoided. 'Mite', when pleased, showers blessings and benefits on people, whereas when they are displeased or enraged, they cause illness, failure of crops, damage to houses or village by storms, lightning or other natural calamities. When the 'spirit bites' the Garos says 'mite chika' which is a symptom of diseases or calamities indicating the spirit that causes them and the kind of actions or sacrifices to be performed for propitiating the concerned 'mite'—spirit. Garos must, therefore, behave in appropriate ways towards the mite if disaster is not to overtake them. Some crops must not be eaten during ripening of crops; the worship-places in the village (Kimindam) should not be trampled over; they must not enter into a particular area of jungle or forest where the spirit specially resides (Ranggadam); observance of the abstinance day (Salnima) is must because there are some of the acts that displease 'the mite that bite'.

Accordingly, there are various kinds of sacrifices for the propitiation of the spirits in connection with ailments. The forms of sacrifices vary from place to place and person to person concerning the kind of spirits which cause ailments. However, the sacrificial erections or preparations are similar. Throughout the hills, the Garo Animists erect sacrificial bamboos which are specially prepared varying in form according to the spirit to whom the offering is made, which are exactly not to be called altars.

The most common is the Sambasia, which consists of an upright, oblong panel composed of a bamboo frame about four to five feet long and two feet broad, filled in with reeds and the leaves of certain trees. Chorabudi, the spirit is also invoked at its base. The invocation of this spirit is to knowingly stick the bamboo into the ground so as to form an inverted cone about three feet high, filled with earth. Another erection for sacrifice we can find is the 'chekrek'. The 'chekrek' is merely a short bamboo stuck upright in the ground, the top section is splited into narrow strips, which, when splayed outwards and bound with cane, form a conical basket. Sometimes it is also filled with cotton. Another form of this is the 'wa·dambeng chekrek'. This consists of two bamboos lashed together in the form of a cross. The top and horizontal extremities of this cross are opened out into the conical basket as described above. The bamboos are then further scraped so that masses of shaving hang down at intervals. When any offering is made at any of these sacrificial altars the blood of the animal or fowl is smeared over it and some of the hairs or feathers are adhered to the bamboos.

In the villages there are always a number of long bamboos with leaves on, placed upright in the ground and that also mostly in front or close to the houses. These bamboos are scraped in the form of human form and cotton bols or bunches of paddy are hung in the ears which is an idea of an offering either to the dead or the spirits. If the sacrifice or offering is made for the dead it is called memang midang (memang means ghost; midang—bunch of paddy); when the offering is made for the spirit it is called mite-midong (mite-spirit and midong—paddy).

In the village, on the roadside we can constantly find some thing which is a proof of the belief in the efficacy of propitiation by sacrifice. These sacrifices are done for minor ailments. For these sacrifices the straw or reeds are pierced through with a bamboo stake; mud or sand are also placed and few strings are tied to upright bamboo sticks. Sometimes the strings are ornamented with coloured rags and an image giving an impression of the beak of a fowl or duck, blood being sprinkled on it and on surrounding earth. These sacrifices are performed at the roadside where there is a small stream. The exactly same sacrifice was performed in one village. The priest took the rag of a child who was ailing from fever or malaria, placed it on a bamboo stake which was filled with reeds and cotton bols - 'chekrek' at the altar - 'sambasia' at the roadside near a stream. Slaughtering a fowl and sprinkling the blood at the 'sambasia' he chanted the words which to my knowledge could not be easily grasped. He took the water and some food cooked at 'sambasia' and fed the sick after the sacrifice. The child was suffering from high fever and was in delirium and simple treatment by some medicines could have been helpful. However, they refused any medical treatment and solely depended on their belief and practice, that, is the sacrifice to the spirit. The priest said it was the 'spirit of the Stream'—'chiringni mite' was the cause of the illness. I observed all the performances and left the place. After a month it was told that the child had recovered from her illness after prolonged suffering.

Whether or not rational in whatever they believe and practice the Garos always do so firmly and sincerely. This proves that they always practice what they believe. The Garos strongly believe that every man and woman will twice in his or her life-time fall very ill and be in danger of dying. According to their belief one such illness will occur in childhood, and the other at adult age. The first illness is called 'bima rima' (bima-main female or mother and rima-catch) and the second kambepea (kambe-height of growth and pe·a-to break). These two illness must come to everybody as it is inevitable. Some persons die at the first stage and some recover and persevere but die at the second, that is at the stage of 'Kambepea'. But some recover even at the second stage. It is never known in what form these illnesses come. They may come as cholera, smallpox, dysentery, malaria or any other disease, and it seems to depend upon the virulence of the attack, and not on the nature of the malady, whether it is to be classed as one or other of the 'predestined' illnesses.[53]

When it is obvious that an illness is either the 'bima rima' or 'kambepea' an expensive sacrifice has to be offered. Sometimes even pigs and cattle may have to be offered in sacrifice for the recovery of the patient; and in case of a man of wealth, the ceremony becomes one of some importance and the sacrifice is performed by the Kamal-priest as usual over sambasia near the stream. If the matters become worse, an intensive sacrifice, that is 'den·jaringa' ceremony, has to be performed.

For this ceremony a place is cleared near a stream in the jungle. Sambasia is erected together with various bamboo receptacles for offerings of rice, cotton, etc. The officiating 'kamal' or priest sacrifices a fowl, smears its blood over the sambasia and adheres the bird's feathers. He then tries one end of a cotton thread to the sambasia, leads it to the sick man's house and fastens the other end in the room in which he is lying. On the string a spring of kimbal (callicarpa arborea) leaves is hung. The idea is that if the sick man's spirit leaves his body it may be induced to return by the prayers of his friends, and will be able to find its way back by means of the thread as a guide. Outside the house the priest takes up his stand, and during the whole day invokes Tatara-Rabuga to cure the sick person. A horn is continuously blown so that the evil spirit may be frightened away by which the sick man is afflicted. If there is improvement or change in his condition, even at night, the priest addresses his prayers of command to the spirit 'Bidawe', who steals the souls of men, and continues his intercession as before. This is kept up until a late hour; after which the cotton string is examined where the leaves were hung, and if it shows any sign of having sagged, it is believed that the sick man's spirit has come back, and that he will recover. The string is then broken, and a piece of it tied round the neck of the invalid; drums and musical instruments are beaten in the sick room, and his relations begin to rejoice. This was somewhat an awkward feeling for us who never came across such performance. But there is a belief that the deities have heard the prayers giving the sign that the sick will certainly be cured. The beating of drums is done as they believe it will cheer up the patient and buoy him up greatly and that the pandemonium created by the musical instruments in so confined a space creats no harm to the sick.[54]

A· SONGTATA CEREMONY

In addition to the various sacrifices for individual cases of illness, there are certain ceremonies which are observed once a year in connection with ailments. The a·songtata ceremony (a·song land and tata sacrifice) is performed once a year by whole community or village. This is observed in order to safeguard its members from dangers of the forest, sicknesses, diseases and from any other natural calamity during the year. Close to the outskirts of every big village a number of stones may be noticed stuck into the ground. These are known by the name a·song and on them is offered the sacrifice which the A·songtata demands. At first a goat is sacrificed and a month later, that of a langur or a bamboo rat is considered necessary. The animal chosen is fastened by a rope round its neck and is led by two men to every house in the village. It is taken inside each house in turn. Meanwhile, the assembled villager, beating the walls from outside frighten and drive out any evil spirits which may have taken up their residence within. All the houses of the village are covered in the same manner. The monkey or rat is led to the outskirts of the village, slaughtered by one blow of a dao and then crucified on bamboos set up in the ground. Round the crucified animal, long and sharp bamboo stakes are placed, which form *chevaur de frise* round about it. These comemmorate the days when such defences surrounded the villages on all sides to keep off human enemies; they are now a symbol to ward off sickness and dangers to life from wild animals of the forest. The langur required for the purpose is hunted down some days before, but should it be found impossible to catch one, a brown monkey may take its place, but a hulock is not used.

This ceremony is observed by every village of the Garo animists every year. Even at the present time, this is seen in the interior villages, except in the Christian dominated villages.

VII
Religious Content in Funeral Ceremony

BELIEF CONCERNING DEATH

The Garos believe in death and rebirth. According to Garo legends there was no occurrence or incidence of death as such. All the human beings were immortal and death was unknown and never took place. Human beings were placed in a reigning position upon other creatures. According to one of the sayings, in certain period of time one of the family of Garos being bored with the life and wanting some extra-amusement told the Megam - Airipa to act as a dead man. Airipa then pretended to be dead and his family too mourned for him as if he was really dead. The gathered folk then covered the body with the cloth and wailed as if he was really dead. All the neighbours and villagers came and joined in their mourning. Their mourning and wailing was heard by the 'Dakgipa-Rugipa' - the creator deity. The Creator was surprised how the knowledge of *death* was learned by his creatures. Being disappointed by their acting he released the soul of Airipa and took him back. The pretending person then was found really *dead*. It was from that point of time that phenomenon of death came to exist among human beings according to the belief of the Garos. The Megam-Airiipa was the 'first man' who died and all other human beings began to die at appointed time as the creator brought the 'death' upon them. The cause of death then appeared as illness, disease or other natural phenomena.

The Garos also believe that the original dwelling place of the spirits of death was 'Napak'. During the period of their stay in Napak hills, people used to cultivate land together with the ghosts of the dead. There is a legend about the shifting of a dwelling place of the spirits of the dead from Napak to Balpakram which says that one day, while the living man and the dead spirits were cultivating the land together a woman of Napak clan happened to split the stump of a tree from the jhum field for firewood. As soon as the Napak woman splitted a dead stump tree, the spirit of the dead cried out saying that her father was killed, her mother was killed and the land or place is no longer safe for dwelling. "Let us run away from here," saying these words, all the spirits of the dead ran away from Napak to the farthest place of "Balpakram" - the abode of spirits or the land of spirits.[55]

DISPOSAL OF THE DEAD

The Garos usually burn their dead and the cremation takes place at night. However, there are certain exceptions to this rule. As for example, a leper is not burnt but buried. In ancient times the lepers were isolated in huts and kept confined and at the last stage of the disease, they and their huts were burnt down. If a man suffers from incurable disease, he would be left to live alone at the far away interior forest with little or no provision for survival, giving him rice and a few utensils. When the provision is over he dies of starvation.

When some people die of unnatural cause or face immature death their dead bodies are disposed off accordingly. When a person is killed by a tiger or any wild animal, his body is cremated but the cremation takes place in the day time. Moreover, the dead body would not be taken into the village but cremated at the spot where the body was found. Besides, no funeral rites would be conducted for him and his belongings would be destroyed as they consider that it is taboo to make use of them after such unnatural death. The Garos also believe that the person who is killed by a tiger or any wild animal, his family members or his forthcoming children may also be ill-fated to suffer the same incident if not all atleast one or two. That is why if someone is killed by tiger or wild animal the Garos say that perhaps someone of his forefathers might have been killed in the same way. If someone escapes from the attempt of a tiger or wild elephant he or she is renamed believing that he or she will still be a target. Same thing is believed even in the case of suicides—that someone of the family members or clan may follow the same process of death. In this connection the Garos always are careful and try to get clear knowledge of the clan and its past history into which one is going to get married.

When a person dies, the relatives are all informed of it. If the relatives of the deceased live nearby, then the cremation takes place immediately, but if the relatives live at distant places then the dead body is kept undisposed even for two to three days, though the dead body begins to decompose. The relatives and friends who are at the nearby village immediately collect at the house of the deceased person as soon as the news of a death is heard. The visitors and relatives come with rice-filled of kerang (the garo basket) and other things like tobacco, chilli, ginger, etc. necessary for cooking at the house of the deceased and as an assistance to the family of the deceased. The nearest relative or the next elder or eldest of the deceased comes with a cow, rice, and a degchi of rice beer and on reaching the house signals by a blank fire of a gun or musket. This is also done by the great uncles of the deceased or the clan-mahari. People who gather are then busy in killing cows and cooking. Some of the men prepare the alter for cremation. Women stay with the corpse wailing.

Before cremation, the dead body is placed on a row of gongs and other valuables if the dead person happens to be of a rich family; but the corpse of a poor man is laid down upon the bamboo floor. The body is then washed with undiluted liquor if he is rich, but with water if he is poor. The washing is done by the nearest relative, that is the aunt, cousin or sister or the mother of the deceased person. According to the custom some gongs or any valuable material like plates made of brass are given to the person who washes the corpse as the customary practice.

The women of the family along with the priest keep watch over the dead body which is kept for about two days or a night during which the cremation takes place. The priest while watching over the dead body keeps reciting unceasing dirge recalling the good deeds and qualities of the deceased and prays that his spirit may be taken safely to its destination. Usually the wailing of the women contains also an invocation to Megam-Airipa, the first man who died. They also warn the spirit of the dead person to beware of Nawang (the evil spirit) and of the dangers on the way to Chitmang —the hill where Balpakram, the land of spirits, is located, and to return to his relative's or mother's house when released from that place.

The A·kawes, have a little different way of disposing the corpse. According to their custom they march in a procession from the house of the dead to the relatives and to the house of the mother of the deceased before cremation. The Am·bengs instead has the custom of placing the corpse on the funeral pyre by the relation and march in procession round it. The nearest relation holds a bunch of cock's feathers in his hand. They move off to the house of the mother of the deceased and place the feathers on the Kima or the Memorial Post, or lay them in the house until the Kima is curved. In the meantime horns are blown, drums and gongs are beaten as is usual on all solemn occasions. Liquor is an important item on such occasions. This practice is significant as they believe the spirit of the deceased may not be lost on the way to its destination and that it may return to it's mother's house when released from spirit land. This ceremony is known as Ja·ragata or the bringing home of the spirit.

When all the relatives and well wishers have arrived, cremation ceremony takes place. The body is then taken out and placed upon the funeral pyre or altar called *Ganchi*. This is built in the 'atila' or public square of the village, in front of, and close to the house of mourning. The Ganchi is built with four upright posts, in a rectangle shape and filled with logs of wood. These posts are sometimes roughly carved. A sort of ornamentation of the ganchi is the Mangpil a T-shaped board about two feet long and one foot broad, on which rough pictures of human beings are painted with a mixture of blood and soot. One such ornament is hung on each of the four sides of the ganchi, and they remain there until the pile of wood is set on fire. They are then taken down and kept to hang round the *delang* or shrine.

During cremation, if the body does not burn well, it is believed that the Nawang has got hold of the spirit of the deceased, and so some brass earings are thrown on the fire as an offering to induce him to release it.

For burning a body certain trees are not used. The most favourite wood is the mandal tree (Erythrina

Suberosa). It is believed that if the corpse is burned with common wood which is considered as bad wood the spirit in its re-incarnation will have bad health. Some woods are not used at all. For example, the cotton-tree is believed to bring bad luck to the spirit; the boldak (Schima Walichii) causes itching and interferes with the spirit's rest; the agatchi (Dilennia Pentagyna) causes sorrow and tears, for it is full of water or sap. A hard wood is prefered, for it is thought that the flame of such wood is of greater help to the spirit than that of softer fuel.[56]

The bull which is kept tethered to a Y-shaped post named galmirong is slaughtered when the last of the body is about to be consumed by the fire, and this animal will accompany the spirit which will be of service for the dead person in the next world. The relatives of the deceased bring several animals which are made to fight before being sacrificed. The victorious bull is then thought to be of much honour of the owner. It is also believed that all the bulls or cows which are brought to the house of the deceased must be killed for the purpose for which they are brought. If any of them is kept and reared, it won't survive and another death may occur in the same family. The same incident as such was witnessed in one of the areas of Selsela village, where many bulls and cows were brought to the house of the death by the close and neighbouroing relatives. All of them were killed one by one leaving not even one, though surprisingly the meat could not be consumed by the gathered folk. It is due to the ancient belief that such killing was done though the familly and the deceased person by now belonged to christianity.

In some parts, a dog is supposed to guide the spirit to Chitmang. The animal is killed and placed under the Ganchi and burned with the corpse.

In olden times the human sacrifice was common and customary. A living slave was also tied to the leg of the corpse from the day of the death to the hour of cremation. For human sacrifice they used to go to hunt from another village and not from their own village. If they failed to bring the human being alive, they brought the head and burned it at the cremation. This created an enmity between one village and another. Therefore, this human sacrifice was abandoned and the bull took its place.

On the next day of the cremation, the widow, widower or a near relation of the deceased, goes to the place of cremation with a cooking pot, some rice, fresh-water prawns, and an egg. These are cooked, if possible, on the embers of the funeral fire, and when the food is ready, the mourner lamenting loudly breaks the vessel. The food is given with an intention that the spirit may be strengthened while travelling. This food which is specially served is called Mi-memang or Ghost Rice. The rice represents usual food of living person, the prawns are cooked because when the ghost of Megam-Airipa, the first man who died, returned to his home, he found his wife catching prawns; and the egg represents the wakmil or fat pig eaten at the funeral feast.

The remaining bones are also collected carefully from the ashes. The ashes collected in a basket are taken into the jungle and deposited there. It is not emptied, but carefully placed on the ground and left. The disposal of the bones differs from place to place and according to the divisions among the Garos. Among the A·kawes we find that they place the bone in a pot wrapped in a cloth and kept on a chekrek, a corn shaped pot made of bamboo. Then it is lashed to the maljuri post of the deceased's house. A small cloth canopy, called Alang, is spread over the bones, and a notched stick fixed so as to represent steps from the floor to the pot. It is believed that this is to enable the spirit of the dead to return to the bones should it wish to do so. A daily offering of food like rice and curry is made to the bones until the post funeral ceremony has been performed.

The Am·bengs and Chisaks also collect the bones in similar way and kept in a pot but they bury the pot in the earth outside the deceased's house. Delang or shrine is built over the pot and food is offered.

About two months after the cremation ceremony, the second ceremony takes place. Among the A·kawes, the pot is brought out of the house and taken to a place where preparations have been made for feasting and dancing. The bones are distributed among some of the female relatives of the deceased, who carry them and dance during the entire celebrations. Finally, the bones are taken to the jungle and buried there.

The Am·bengs also do the same feasting and dancing after which the Delang is set on fire but the bones are not taken out.

The Atongs follow similar ways of collecting the bones like Am·bengs. They also bury the bones of the dead and erect a Delang over them, but during the second ceremony they dig out the bones and dance with them like A·kawes.

The Rugas and the Chiboks vary somewhat from other divisions of the tribe in the manner of conducting their funeral ceremonies. Like all other Garos they burn their dead. The Rugas then bury the bones like the Am·bengs, but instead of erecting a Delang over them, they cover them over with a winnowing-tray made of bamboo. A long bamboo is stuck into the ground by the side and a strip of white cloth is attached which floats in the air like a pennant. Food and drink are offered to this as the other Garos do.

In the post-funeral ceremony, the women put on peculiar silver ornaments called penta, and solemn dance takes place in memory of the dead. After the ceremony is over, the bamboo and the tray are set on fire and destroyed without disturbing the bones.

The post-funeral ceremony of the Chiboks differs from that of Rugas. Among the Chiboks, after the cremation, the bones and ashes are collected and thrown away. A Gelek or small round stool made of bamboo is placed at the foot of the Maljuri—the main post in the house of the deceased. This is intended to be the seat for the spirit in case it returns. In the second ceremony, four bamboos are set up so as to mark out a square. A fowl is killed and its blood smeared on the bamboos. Some valuable ornaments are hung up between the posts where the stool is placed in the middle of the square after which the whole collection is set on fire.

The Chiboks used to plant the branch of the Mandal tree (Erythrina Suberosa) both after the cremation and after the post-funeral ceremony. The plantation of the Mandal tree is done by the side of the principal path to the village, signifying that several deaths had taken place in a Chibok village. The horns of the bulls, sacrificed during the funeral, are also fastened to the trees.

The post-funeral ceremony mentioned above is called Delang So·a (Delang means shrine, and So·a means to burn) by the Ambengs and Mangona or Mangroa by other Garos.

The Christians, however, do not burn their dead. They bury them and the funeral ceremony is performed. The post funeral ceremonies are conducted only in certain areas, mostly in the plain areas among the a.kawes, chiboks, duals, etc., and that also according to the Christian practices involving certain customary principles.

The Garos worship and their various festivals and ceremonies discussed above make up their religion notably varying from place to place and according to the sub-tribes. The Garo tribal religion consisting of the various ceremonies and observances is fast disappearing even among the animists due to the modernisation and progress in education. This study, though not in detail, contains the central beliefs and practices of the tribal Garos which is philosophical and highly valuable for the future studies.

VIII
Life After Death

The Garos believe in life after death. The soul of the dead goes to the appointed place after death. The spirit is believed to be in the abode of ghosts—Balpakram. The departed soul of the death is believed to remains even after the death. When the post-funeral ceremony is performed, the spirit is said to be released. Then, the 'Nawang' accompanies the spirit to its appointed place, that is, the Abode of Spirits or the Land of Spirits—called Balpakram. The spirits are believed to be in the Balpakram for certain period of years until unless they are incarnated or re-born.

Balpakram, the land of spirits, as believed by the Garos, is full of legends, lores, myths and beliefs. It stands at the height of about 3000 ft. above sea level. Balpakram hill is a beautiful site to behold in the early hour of the morning with the rays of sun casting their refulgence light up to the Chitmang hills. The sunset is also can be viewed spectacularly along with the splendor of these beautiful hills. It is situated away from human habitation in the South-Eastern part of South Garo Hills district, occupying an important place in Garo mythology and at present it is one of the National Parks or the Animal Sanctuary.[57]

'Balpakram' is defined in many ways with different meanings by different authors and writers or ancestors. Etymologically the word 'Balpakram' comes from two words: 'Balpaka' which means 'carried away by wind' and 'ram' which means 'the place or spot'. 'Ram' is a suffix for relating the incidents taking place time to time, Balpakram means a place carried away by wind.

Some of the related legends about the etymological concepts of the origin of the word 'Balpakram' are reproduced below :

Shri. Mijendro Sangma, Rambil gittim (Mahadeo) related the story as the present Balpakram was known as 'Kundulgop'. One day, a man was passing through this hill carrying a basketful of chillies, brinjals etc. to his home. Suddenly, a strong wind carried him down the precipice and he was killed. Since then the people called this place 'Balpakram' or a place carried by wind.[58]

Jefferson K. Sangma, Kharkutta, East Garo Hills, also says that the word, 'Balpakram' was there from time immemorial. One day, one lady named Madi was coming to the market carrying a basketful of brinjals, chillies, pumpkins etc. and was passing through this hill. Suddenly, a strong wind blew her away down the deep canyon and she was killed. From that time onwards, the place was known as, 'Balpakram' or the place blown by strong wind.[59]

The most accurate meaning of the word 'Balpakram' is the place of cool breeze blowing incessantly. The Balpakram hill is also known as, 'Balkol' or the place from where the wind blows. It is also known as 'Mangru - Mangram A·song' or 'More - A·song - Mode - Chiga' (the land of the spirits of the dead).

Nelson Marak, village Masighat Agimpal, South Garo Hills, says that the word 'Balpakram' originates from the fact that one day a group of six young men and six young girls were going to 'chugan' festival or death ceremony across this mountain. Suddenly a strong cyclone swept away these twelve youth and they were killed. Henceforth, this place came to be known as 'Balpakram' or the place blown away by the strong wind.[60]

From the above narration we are able to draw the meaning of Balpakram worthy of the present beliefs of the Garos. 'Balpakram' as the abode of Ghosts or the Land of the Spirits, is a mysterious land with legends and mythological spots, streams, caves, stones, medicinal plants, and beautiful orchids.

Towards the sunset at the point of dusk all kinds of cries like howling of jackals, barking of dogs, crying of children, singing and shouting of human voices can be heard. These cries and the noises are of the spirits who live there after the death.

It is also believed that the spirits which live there cultivate the land and plant all kinds of crops as they do when they are alive. That is why seeds of all kinds of crops like rice, millet, melons, ginger, brinjal etc. are presented to the spirits of the dead at the time of death ceremony so that they can cultivate and plant them in their next life at Balpakram. It is also found that certain stones which can be found in Balpakram are imprinted with the images of human footprints and all kinds of seeds like rice, millets, brinjals, pumkins, melons, maize, etc.

The spirits are said to live in the Balpakram for certain period of time, for about twenty years before they are incarnated. There is a belief amongst the Garos that the spirit, Almighty, the giver of life after death lives at Chitmang hill near Balpakram. This spirit, the Giver of life and death, is known as 'Waimong' and looks after every human being on earth and has the power to create and destroy human souls. Accordingly, the spirits are reborn at his will.

RE-INCARNATION

One of the most interesting superstitions which exists among the beliefs of Garos is the subject of Re-incarnation. They believe that when the spirits reach their destination, that is, the abode of ghosts or Balpakram also called Mangru-Mangram a kind of purgatory, they are to look for their relations who have gone before them. They also build the houses and live with their relatives who have not returned to the earthly life. Spirit land is not in any sense a place of joy, and a speedy release with a happy re-incarnation is hoped for.

The Garos also believe that with the birth of every child a spirit leaves purgatory. Therefore, sumptuous and honourable ceremony is performed for the death during funeral and at post-funeral ceremony. Every dead body is marked with the blood of the slaughtered bull or cow at funeral ceremony with the expectation that they may be born in the same clan, family or near relatives. In this connection, an incident was related by Jenseng Sangma that, after the death of their first born male child, another of the same sex having a red patch on the forehead was delivered by his wife's sister in another village.[60]

Another case, according to the statement of Shri. Tonggan Marak of Gimbegri, was that of the wife of Tonggan about to deliver a baby. At the night of ailment for delivery, she dreamt that her grandfather, who was living with her sister in different village came to her house to live with them. Then, she delivered a baby boy towards the dawn. After some moments the news of the death of her grandfather was received. The belief was that the spirit of Tonggan's wife's grandfather was re-incarnated in the same family. This is one of the many beliefs that the spirits of some dead people are directly re-incarnated without reaching the abode of spirits.[61]

There is a belief that in some cases the spirit has the power of leaving the body before death and of entering into another body. Certain ailments are attributed to the fact that the sufferer's spirit cannot make up its mind where to stay, and is therefore restless and uneasy. When this is the case, the person, whose soul is afflicted, becomes thin and emaciated; and if he dies, it is believed that the spirit has entered the body of a child which is yet unborn. Should the afflicted person recover (by some rituals or sacrifice), for certain rituals or sacrifices are performed for such cases, some woman will bear a dead child. If the case is that the afflicted person does not recover the case of bearing a dead child will not occur.

The length of the term of probation at Balpakram and the manner of the return to earth greatly depends on the case of the person's death, or upon the sins he committed during life-time, or the performance of the funeral ceremony. For instance, it is believed that if the person commits suicide by hanging, his or her spirit will be re-incarnated in the form of a beetle, which is condemned to eat nothing but the sap or gum of the plant from which the fibre is obtained to make the rope.

The spirits of the dead killed by the elephant, tiger or any other animal, which go to the abode of spirit Chitmang or Balpakram, are re-incarnated in the form of the animal which caused the death. In no way they will return to the earth in the form of human being. The spirit of the murderer is condemned to reside at Chitmang for seven generations before returning to human form. In the cases of the death of the people with sins committed while alive they are punished by being born in the form of animals. However after the death of the animal they may be re-incarnated in the form of human being if the spirit of the animal reaches the Chitmang. The performance of the funeral rites are taken as most important. If the funeral rites are not performed the spirit does not go to the Chitmang, the abode of spirits, instead, it winds away on earth and turns to evil spirit and re-incarnation is of little hope. Even in the next life it is made slave of other spirits and if re-incarnated at all, it is born to be poor and has to live a hard life on earth. It is also thought that the spirit loses the way to the Chitmang and therefore loses its opportunity and the way to return to the same clan, family or relative at in-carnation. It appears from this that the spirits of animals are like the souls of men, and are supposed to go to the Balpakram as the funeral rites prove that this is the Garo belief. There are many folklores and legends regarding such beliefs.

All these beliefs and superstitions of the Garos as regards the life after death and re-incarnation resemble the beliefs and practice of Hinduism, Buddhism or any other religions which follow the same thread of belief.

ACULTURATION

The beliefs and practices of the Garo Tribal Religion are now been disappearing rapidly. The Garo animists are becoming a minority group. As many Garos have been converted to Christianity, they have abandoned the rituals or ceremonies connected to the jhum cultivation, ailments and funeral ceremonies. However, the Garos cannot completely be free from certain beliefs, superstitions and cultural and traditional practices which are inborn in their minds.

The belief in dreams still is very important as it is important in the O·pata ceremony in Jhum Cultivation. The Garo animists do not eat certain fruits before the Wangala ceremony without first offering to the spirit. In the same way even among the Christians it is found that they don't eat any fruits or rice or millets, without first offering them for the church. The traditional dresses and ornaments are still preserved well in some houses. The cultural dance 'Wangala' is performed during the church services and other functions with little modification. The traditional dresses and ornaments are worn with more beautification; beating the drums, blowing of flutes, etc. remain part of the Garo culture. The belief in certain musical instruments like the Rang, Kram - the Gongs, is still maintained as they are sacred and are not simply touched or beaten because they can cause certain illness by the bite of the spirit - 'Mite Chika'.

To preserve the basic religious principles and the cultural dances, the celebration of the Hundred Drums, 'Wangala' Festival is held every year sometimes in between October and November. The accurate ceremony of Wangala is displayed during this festival in front of honourable chief guests and distinguished people. Some indigenous articles are also exhibited. The competition of Wangala dances from various villages take part in this festival and indigenous games are also conducted. All the youth irrespective of caste, creed and sex can participate in these games.

The beliefs which are still found among the Garos are the beliefs about birth and death. Even the Christians Garos, still believe in the illness called 'Bima rima'- the sickness or illness which takes place from age zero year to six years or more and the Kambe Pea, which takes place between ten years and twenty years of age. The belief that 'every Garo must fall ill at least two times in his life time is still there'. However, no ceremony or ritual is performed for the sickness among the Christians. Instead they consult the Oja— the Garo physician who can treat the illness.

Belief in the funeral ceremony also is still found among the Christian Garos, that unless and until the funeral ceremony is performed the spirit of the dead will not reach its destination. However, the funeral ceremony is performed according to the Christian rites. The traditional practice of killing of bulls, cows, etc. for the spirit of the dead is found in some villages where, though they may be Christians, their traditional custom is still maintained.

Among the plain Garos like Rugas, Chiboks and Chisaks or A·kawes the post funeral ceremony is performed. That ceremony is similar to that of Hindu's 'shraad,' or Memang kam as it is commonly called where the bulls, cows, pigs etc. are slained for the spirit of the dead. The prayer services or condolence service is conducted in Christian way.

From all these beliefs and practices we can trace the aculturation among the Garos. The traditional beliefs and practices are still inherent in the mind of the Garos.

IX
Conclusion

The content of the study is limited to the centre of beliefs and practices of the ancient Garo Sangsareks who practised what they believed. There are many more things to be written and kept in record for the future generations. Some of the religious practices are now being simply neglected as the knowledgeable people who would have narrated them have passed away. So study deals with the centre of beliefs and practices of the Garo Tribals in their day-to-day lives. Though their ancient beliefs and practices are now disappearing due to the christianisation, in many parts of the Garo Hills this Tribal Religion is practised even at the present time.

The belief in the Deities is one of the strong beliefs among the Garo Tribals as all the ceremonies discussed above are concerned with the consultation with them and their help. The belief in the dreams is fundamental which is very significant for the Garo Sangsareks as well as the Christians. The importance of the belief in the dreams is clearly seen in the first ceremony of the Jhum cultivation, that if one happens to have bad dream he abandons the plot of land which he intends to cultivate. But if one dreams of plenty of sand collected in his front house, it signifies that one will be getting plenty of paddy in his cultivation. Besides the beliefs in dreams in connection with the jhumming there are other superstitions regarding dreams. For example, if one dreams of building a new house then it is believed that he or she or some one of his or her near relative is likely to die. If one happens to dream about catching plenty of fish, he or she is likely to get plenty of money or prosperous life is indicated. Dreaming of bathing in the dirty water indicates ill heath or serious sickness. If one happens to dream of getting married himself or herself then also it is believed that one may fall sick. If one dreams of his or her engagement it is believed that one may be beaten by the tiger if he or she goes to the jungle on the following day. If one goes to the deep river or stream it is believed to be taken by the mermaid. The dreamer then tries to abstain from going out anywhere. Death for the dreamer or his relations is presaged in a number of ways. To dream of cutting hair means that a bear will kill the dreamer, while to dream of falling stone indicates a fatal blow from an elephant's tusk. The breaking of right tooth in dream is a warning of death for the dreamer. These examples could be indefinitely multiplied, for each division of tribe has its own ideas on the subject, and its own interpretations.

The Garos are so implicit as believers in the warnings and promises conveyed in dreams, that they are by no means content to accept an evil dream. They try to avert the misfortune which the dreams foretell. The ceremony called *'Tatpronga' is* performed in order to avert the evil. The manner in which this ceremony is performed after a bad dream, the dreamer goes into the jungle and collects a handfull of brooms called 'simu' and keeps it till the next morning, waiting for the Kamal who comes to the house with an appointment at sunrise. The two then go out together to the right-hand corner of the dreamer's house (if the dreamer is a woman they go to the left-hand corner on going out), and there the priest-Kamal strikes the dreamer on both sides of the body with the simu, repeating certain exorcisms the while. The two then go to the nearest stream carrying a cock with them. The cock is killed and its blood allowed to fall into a little boat made from banana stem. The boat is then floated away in the stream, and while the water carries away the boat the dreamer bathes himself in the stream. The underlying symbolic meaning is that the spirits having been appeased by the prayers of the priest, the chastisement of the dreamer, and the sacrifice of the fowl, the boat is allowed to bear away with it the *marang* or ill-luck which the dream portended.

The religious content in the Garo marriage ceremony called, DO·SIA is one of the practices among the Garo Tribal religious people. In the do·sia ceremony, the bridegroom side is asked to bring the cock and the bride side is asked to bring the hen. The priest then beats up both of them and by killing the chickens looks at the intestines. The right-side of the intestine is assigned to bride and groom and their health. The leftside of the intestine is assigned to the deity-mite. If the right intestine overlaps the left one it is believed to be good omen; if it happens to be opposite then it indicates bad omen. If the right intestine is longer than the left one and full of black dung it indicates good health as well as prosperous life of the couple; if vice-versa the indication is ill health, poverty and one of them may be short lived. This belief in looking at and predicting by intestine of chickens is not only done in marriage ceremony alone, but one who is knowledgeable, practices this to know the luck of any person who comes as a guest or stranger to his house.

Besides the religious beliefs, the Garos also have certain superstitious beliefs that death can be caused by a simple process of practicing a kind of snippings. The beliefs in the witchcraft, magic, sorceries, ghosts, etc., are common among them.

ENDNOTES

1. Milton S. Sangma pp. 3-5, *History and Culture of the Garos.*
2. Imperial Gazetteer of India, 1909 p. 504.
3. Tiger-men is a case of psycho-physical transformation, which is a fundamental belief and practice, in which a human being is seen in different images as tiger, elephant, pig, etc., and when adepts or shamans, through their own non-human alter egos, and adept's alter ego, as a tiger happens to be in particular area of jungle near human habitation, the self same tiger clearly understands human talks and gossips.

   Ibid; JADORENG (the psycho-physical culture of the Garos)

   Ch.II : Psycho-Physical Transformation of Human Beings into Non-Human Earthly Living Beings.

   Dewansing Rongmithu Sangma.
4. Playfair, A; '*The Garos*,' pp. 8-14.
5. Milton S. Sangma, '*Hill Societies*', pp. 200.
6. Dr. M. Sangma, *Hill Societies*, pp. 200.
7. M.C. Thomas, *Hill Societies; Religions and Customs Among the Garos*, pp. 201.
8. Major Playfair; *The Garos*, pp. 80
9. Sinha, T.; *The Psyche of Garos*, p. 47.
10. M.C. Thomas., '*Religions Beliefs and Customs Among the Garos*', p. 201.

11. L.P. Vidyarthi Binay Kumar Rai, *The Tribal Culture of India*, pp. 236.
12. M.S. Sangma; *History and Culture of the Garos*, pp. 220.
13. Ibid.
14. Playfair; *The Garos*, pp. 80
15. Robbins Burling; *Rengsanggri*, pp. 54-55.
16. n. 14, p. 81.
17. Rongmithu, D.S.; *Apasong Agana* (Our Forefathers tell us), p. 198.
18. n. 16.
19. Sangma D.K.; *Folklore, Part III*, pp. 24-25.
20. Sangma S. Milton, *History and Culture of the Garos*.
21. n. 16.
22. n. 20, p. 222.
23. n. 16.
24. n. 20, p. 223.
25. n. 20, p. 224.
26. Burling, Robbins, *Rengsanggri*, p. 59.
27. n. 24, p. 223.
28. n. 14, p. 82.
29. Sinha, T., *The Psyche of the Garos*, p. 52.
30. n. 19, p. 28.
31. n. 25.
32. n. 20, pp. 61, 62.
33. Sangma, J., Principles of Garo Law, pp. 23-24.
34. n. 26, pp. 223-24.
35. n. 20, p. 64.

36. Nakane, Chie; *Garo Khasi-Comparative Study in Matrilineal Systems*, p. 61.
37. *Ibid.*, p. 14.
38. n. 26, pp. 228-29.
39. Marak Marak, K. R, *The Garos and their Customary Laws and Usages*, p. 23
40. n. 20, p. 66.
41. n. 14, p. 98.
42. Playfair, p. 98.
43. Mihir N. Sangma, *Maniani Bidik* (The Core of Religious Beliefs).
44. n. 26, p. 68.
45. Mihir N. Sangma, *Maniani Bidik*, (The Core of Religious Beliefs), pp. 7, 8.
46. Ibid, p. 9.
47. n. 20, p. 240 : Also vide, Sangma, N; Mihir : Maniani Bidik. p. 9.
48. n. 26, p. 62.
49. n. 20, pp. 24-42.
50. n. 45, pp. 17-19.
51. n. 20, p. 181.
52. Fr. G. Costa's Code of Law, (Chap. XXIX p. 29.)
53. n. 14, p. 90.
54. n. 14, pp. 91, 92.
55. Julius L. R. Marak, *Balpakram The Land of Spirits*, p. 37.
56. n. 14, p. 94, 95.
57 Julius R. Marak : *Balpakram*, p. 35.

58. Shri. Mijendro Sangma, vill. Rambilgittim, Mahadeo, South Garo Hills, on 20-08-1996, Julius R. Marak; Balpakram, p. 36.
59. Shri. Jefferson K. Sangma, vill. Upp. Kharkutta, E. Garo Hills, on 26. 6. 96 and 31.7.96. Ref. Julius R. Marak; Balpakram, p. 36.
60. Julius R. Marak, Balpakram, p. 37.

Bibliography

1. Flayfair, Major A, *The Garos.*
2. Sangma, S Milton, *History and Culture of the Garos.*
3. Vidyarthi, P.L. and Raikumar, Miray, *The Tribal Culture of India.*
4. Sangma Rongmithu, Dewansing, Jadoreng (*the psychophysical culture of the Garos*)
5. Sangma Rongmithu, Dewansing, *Folk Tales.*
6. Sangma Rongmithu, Dewansing, *Epiclores of the Garos.*
7. Sangma Rongmithu, Dewansing, *Apasong Agana.*
8. Sangma N. Mihir, *Pagitchamni Ku·bisring.*
9. Burling, Robins, *Rengsanggri.*
10. Sinha, A, *The Psyche of the Garos.*
11. Choudory, P.N., *Linguistic and Cultural Aspect of the Garos.*
12. Sangma N. Mihir, *Maniani Bidik.*
13. Costa, Guilio (Fr), *The Garo Code of Law.*
14. Marak R, Julius, *Garo Customary Law and Practices.*
15. Marak R, Julius, *Balpakram.*
16. Sangma S. Milton, *History of Garo Literature.*
17. Carey, William, *The Garo Jungle Book.*
18. Chandra Kar, Parimal (M.Com, MA, Ph.D), *Glimpses of the Garos.*
19. Gassah, L.S, *Garo Hills Land and the People.*

20. L.R. Marak, Julius, *Balpakram (The Land of Spirits) Garos Mythology*.
21. Sangma S. Milton, *Hill Societies: Their Modernation* (A study of Northeast with special reference to Garo Hills).

Index

T

W